DISCARDED

Aboriginal Legends of Canada

Cree

Megan Cuthbert

Weigl

Published by Weigl Educational Publishers Limited
6325 10th Street SE
Calgary, Alberta T2H 2Z9

Website: www.weigl.ca

Library and Archives Canada Cataloguing in Publication available upon request.
Fax 403-233-7769 for the attention of the Publishing Records Department.

ISBN 978-1-77071-560-8 (hardcover)
ISBN 978-1-77071-561-5 (softcover)
ISBN 978-1-77071-562-2 (multi-user eBook)

Printed in the United States of America in North Mankato, Minnesota
1 2 3 4 5 6 7 8 9 0 17 16 15 14 13

072013
WEP130613

Project Coordinator: Heather Kissock
Editor: Alexis Roumanis
Designer: Mandy Christiansen
Illustrator: Martha Jablonski-Jones

Photo Credits
Weigl acknowledges Alamy and Getty Images as its primary image suppliers for this title.

We acknowledge the financial support of the Government of Canada through the Canada Book Fund for our publishing activities.

CONTENTS

Meet the Cree

The Cree are an **Aboriginal** group that live throughout Quebec, Ontario, Manitoba, Saskatchewan, and Alberta. In the past, the Cree were divided into three different groups. The Woods Cree lived in the northern parts of Saskatchewan and Manitoba. The Plains Cree lived in central Manitoba. The Swampy Cree lived in Manitoba, Ontario, and Quebec. Today, there are about 200,000 Cree in Canada.

Storytelling is important to the Cree. It has allowed their **oral** language to survive. This is because each **generation** tells Cree stories to the next. Cree stories are told during celebrations, ceremonies, and for fun. They are also used to teach important lessons and the history of the Cree people.

Stories of Creation

Many of the stories, or **legends**, told by the Cree explain their history and origins. The Cree have a close relationship with the land. This relationship influences their **spiritual** beliefs. The Cree have several stories that explain how the world and the creatures in it came to be.

The Cree story of O-ma-ma-ma tells of the birth of the world. In the story, it is the spirits and animals that first inhabit Earth. Animals and spirits play a central role in Cree beliefs. The Cree believe that bad luck would come to those who do not respect the spirit world. They perform ceremonies to ask for blessings from the animals they hunt.

Some Cree tell stories using beading. Wampum are beads made from the white and purple shells of quahog clams. The Cree arrange the beads into designs. These designs tell a story.

Deer was one of many animals hunted by the Cree. Deer meat could be used to make stews and soups.

The Plains Cree believed that they could see into the future by looking into water. This technique helped them when hunting and in battle.

The Story of O-MA-MA-MA

In the beginning, the Earth Mother O-ma-ma-ma began giving birth to the spirits of the world. First, she gave birth to Binay-sih, who was a thunderbird. He showed his anger with black clouds, rain, and bolts of fire from the sky.

Next, O-ma-ma-ma gave birth to Ina-kaki. Ina-kaki was a frog who helped control the insects of the world. Then, Wee-sa-hay-jac was born. He was a trickster who could change himself into different forms. The fourth spirit, Ma-heegun, was a little wolf. He would travel with his brother Wee-sa-hay-jac on his back.

Finally, Amik the beaver was born. He was greatly respected by the other spirits because they thought he was a human from another world.

O-ma-ma-ma then gave birth to fish, rocks, grasses, and trees for Earth. For a very long time, Earth was only inhabited by animals and spirits. There were no humans until Wee-sa-hay-jac made people from the earth.

Nature Stories

The Cree's relationship with the land influences many of their beliefs. To the Cree, spirits live throughout the land. These spirits help to guide the Cree in their everyday lives. Many Cree stories explain how the spirits speak to them. Some of these stories also describe **phenomena** that occur in the **natural world**.

Who Calls? is a story about the Qu'Appelle Valley in Saskatchewan. The story describes a haunting echo that the Cree have heard sound throughout the valley for many years. *Who Calls?* tells how this echo became the name of the valley. In doing so, the story also shows the connection between the spirit world and nature.

In the past, the Cree built teepees out of bison hide. They used to tell stories inside their teepees.

Members of the Plains Cree have lived in the Qu'Appelle Valley for hundreds of years. The area was ideal hunting ground for bison, which were a main part of their diet.

Who Calls?

One night, a Cree warrior was canoeing down a river on his way to visit his girlfriend. As he paddled, he thought he heard his name being called.

"Kâ-têpwêt?" he called out, asking "Who calls?" in Cree. There was no reply. He repeated his question in French, saying "Qu'appelle?" Still, there was no answer to his question.

The warrior continued his journey. Further down the river, he again heard his name being called. He thought it sounded like the voice of his girlfriend. He called out, but all he heard in response was the echo of his own voice.

When the warrior finally arrived at his girlfriend's village, he found a crowd gathered around her home. The villagers told the warrior that his girlfriend had fallen sick during the night. Before dying, she had called out his name twice. The warrior ran back to his canoe and began paddling back up the river, calling out "Qu'appelle?" His voice can still be heard echoing through the Qu'Appelle Valley.

Life Lessons

Some Cree stories are told to teach lessons. They often use animals or characters to show people how to act or to explain what happens when someone makes a bad decision. Although many of these stories are told with humour, they send a serious message about how to treat others.

Cree stories are told during celebrations and ceremonies. One type of celebration is the powwow. Besides storytelling, these gatherings also include dancing, games, and craft making.

Ghost Stallion reminds the Cree of the important role horses once played in their lives and encourages them to treat the animals with the respect they deserve. The Cree were introduced to the horse when Europeans began arriving in the region. The animals quickly became a part of Cree life. They played a key role in hunting. A fast horse could help a man collect food quickly and feed more people.

The horse is used in many Cree designs and is an important animal in Cree storytelling.

Horses represented power and wealth to the Cree.

GHOST STALLION

Long ago, there was a wealthy chief who had many horses. However, the chief only loved the young and beautiful horses. Once the horses became old or sick, he would treat them badly. Among his herd was an old white stallion with crooked legs. The chief was upset with the ugly stallion and began hitting it. He left the horse lying in pain.

When the chief returned to see the white stallion, the horse had disappeared. That night, the white stallion appeared to the chief in a dream. The stallion had transformed into the most beautiful horse the chief had ever seen. The stallion told him "Because you were cruel to me, I will take away all the horses you have."

The next morning, the chief awoke to find all of his horses gone. That night, the stallion returned to the chief in his dream, telling him where he could find the horses. When the chief awoke, he followed the stallion's directions, but his horses were not there. This continued night after night, and the chief became thin and sickly. He continues to wander, searching for his lost horses.

Heroic Tales

The Cree often told legends about important people or heroes who displayed qualities that the Cree people respected. Often, these heroes would have to use their skills and **intelligence** to overcome obstacles.

The story of Kuikuhâchâu tells of the quick-thinking man who managed to defeat a great enemy of the people, the Giant Skunk. Kuikuhâchâu shows great leadership and intelligence. These qualities help him protect his family from harm.

Many North American Aboriginal groups have stories about the skunk. It is often portrayed as a monster that a hero must conquer.

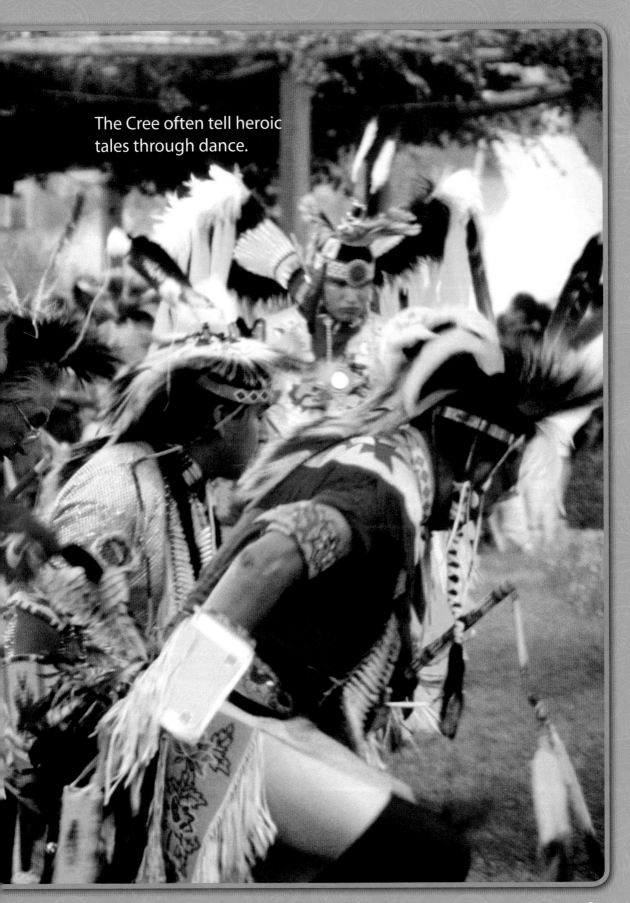

The Cree often tell heroic tales through dance.

The LEGEND of KUIKUHÂCHÂU

Wâniyûyâu was a Giant Skunk who would use his deadly stench to kill people and animals. No one could kill Wâniyûyâu. Everyone lived in fear of him.

One day, one of Kuikuhâchâu's brothers crossed the path of Wâniyûyâu. Kuikuhâchâu was afraid that the skunk would come after them, so he took his family away from their camp.

Wâniyûyâu was still able to find them, however. Kuikuhâchâu was digging a hole in the ice when he heard the skunk approaching. Wâniyûyâu demanded that Kuikuhâchâu turn around to face him, but Kuikuhâchâu would not. When Wâniyûyâu turned to spray Kuikuhâchâu with his deadly scent, Kuikuhâchâu jumped into the hole in the ice, avoiding the spray. When the giant skunk turned around to see his work, Kuikuhâchâu called his brothers over. Together, they attacked the beast and brought it to its death.

Cree 21

Activity

Make Your Own Wampum

You can make your own wampum using noodles and cardboard.

You Will Need:

short, thin noodles

strainer

vinegar

empty coffee can

cardboard

paper towel

red and blue food dye

glue

1. Pour half of the noodles into the empty coffee can.

2. Cover the noodles with vinegar, and add the red and blue food colouring to dye the pasta purple.

3. Strain the pasta, and let it dry on the paper towel.

4. Use the purple and plain noodles to create a design.

5. Glue the noodles in place on the cardboard.

Further Research

Many books and websites provide information on Aboriginal legends. To learn more about this topic, borrow books from the library, or search the internet.

Books

Most libraries have computers that connect to a database for researching information. If you input a key word, you will be provided with a list of books in the library that contain information on that topic. Nonfiction books are arranged numerically, using their call number. Fiction books are organized alphabetically by the author's last name.

Websites

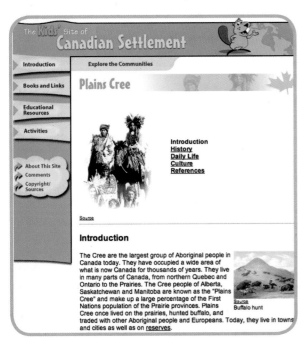

For information on the traditional life of the Cree, visit: www.collectionscanada.gc.ca/settlement/kids/021013-2161-e.html

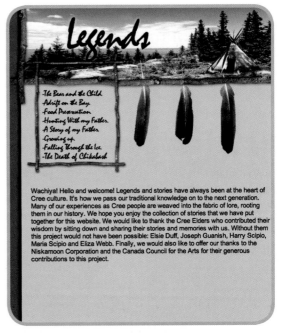

Listen to more Cree legends at: www.beesum-communications.com/english/legends/index.html

Key Words

Aboriginal: First Nations, Inuit, and Métis of Canada

generation: all the people born and living at about the same time

intelligence: the ability to think, learn, and understand

legends: stories that have been passed from generation to generation

natural world: relating to things that have not been made by people

oral: by word of mouth, spoken

phenomena: an unusual fact or event

spiritual: of or related to sacred matters

Index